Jean-Philippe Lecat

BEAUNE

«Can we escape from Beaune if once we have crossed the magic circle
of its ancient mediaeval battlements, dented with bastions, flanked with towers,
bristling with bartizans ? Can we get back to its Saint-Nicholas' Gate when we have lost our way
in its maze of Hell and Paradise streets or its parapet walks with their dead ends and stairways to trap you ?
Beaune la Jolie and Beaune la Vineuse conspire to take you up in their adorned and perfumed arms.»
Pierre Poupon, *Toute la Bourgogne*, PUF, 1970

Photographs : Hervé Champollion
Translation : John Lee

ÉDITIONS OUEST-FRANCE
13, rue du Breil, Rennes

Secretive Beaune

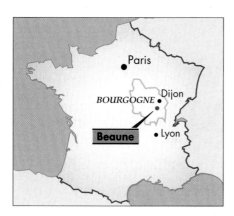

It is never easy to get to know a town, this one probably even less than most. And yet Beaune is very approachable. It has one of the biggest motorway cross-roads in Europe on its doorstep, used by several tens of millions of cars each year.

The Hôtel-Dieu hospital alone attracts over 450,000 visitors. With its noisy crowds, its multicoloured coaches, all the world's languages, the covered marketplace bustles like a major tourist centre. And yet, only a few steps away, the Rue Paradis leads to the apse of the collegiate church on the Place Notre-Dame where time seems to stand still.

Not that Beaune is a museum town. It does have its new neighbourhoods, its industrial estates, its sporting and technical facilities. And most of all, it is a hive of business activity with an international calling ; as the capital of Burgundy, Beaune is at the heart of a powerful web of interests. Its economic importance is out of all proportion with its 22,000 population, since several thousand jobs depend on transactions made within its merchant and export firms. On the third Sunday in November, the Hôtel-Dieu auctions

▽◁ **Left: entrance to the Hôtel-Dieu.**

▽ **Light and peace from the Middle Ages; the cloister of Notre-Dame..**

off the produce of its vineyards. In the mediaeval covered market hung with tapestries from Flanders, the experts listen out for the auctioneer's cries. Two small candles time the auctions. Everything that counts in the world of the vine holds its breath as the dying candle flame starts flickering...

History has made Beaune a secret town. Its finest hotels are protected behind massive doors ; its gardens lie beyond the porches, its carved galleries enclosed to the rear of its courtyards. The high walls of ten convents, the bulwarks of the battlements in the ancient place on the frontier with the Empire, the wrought iron gates protect its inner life. The carefully restored heritage of Beaune is nevertheless placed at the service of present-day activities with the chamber of commerce and industry at the Carmelite convent, government offices at the Ursuline convent and the Hôtel de Montille, the Fine Arts school under the Baronne du Bay's panelling, contemporary painters at the Oratory Chapel etc. But you can stop off at Beaune and hardly see anything of it.

The people of Beaune themselves are slightly stand-offish. There are plenty of scholars, open and welcoming ; the library houses a number of treasures ; erudite societies and active cultural associations act as benevolent guides. The passing visitor is thrilled with the prestige of famous tables, the inexhaustible range of great wines and the quality of the hotels with over a thousand modern rooms. Business relations are handled seriously and competently, whilst the hallmark of human relations is sober reserve, and even a hint of gravity. Like their town, to be appreciated the people of Beaune need the attention that marked out the great travellers of former times.

Even if you only have a few hours to spend in Beaune, you can unravel its secret. Observe the winegrower tasting a «Clos des Mouches», the bees of our Middle Ages. He has not filled a large glass to down at one gulp. He has poured barely a mouthful into his silver wine taster, embossed so as to bring out the wine's colour. His sight, smell and taste all come alive. The entire history of the wine, the flower, the storm and the sun, is revealed to him...

▽ *A dream home, from the Hainault: the Hôtel-Dieu*

The Mysteries of Beaune

«Climates»

The Beaune countryside features three types of landscape : the wildly beautiful limestone plateaux of the Hautes Côtes ; sloping down towards the rising sun, the Côte, which nurtures the famous vineyards ; lastly the Plain, with its crops and forests stretching all the way to the River Saône.

Most of all, it is the meeting of the winds. From the west come the rains and storms. There used to be the harsh old saying : «It's an ill wind and ill folk that come from the Morvan...» The north wind brings frost, which can ruin the entire region in years when it comes late. From the south, the «Saône wind» breathes like a final whiff of the Mediterranean world. The flora and fauna reflect this play of opposite influences ; in July, on «the Mountain», you will both see blue Alpine gentians and hear the cicada from Provence.

Since the 2nd century at least, Beaune judges its weather by the requirements of her vineyards. The tropical creeper from the East, which man's sharp pruning forces to produce bunches charged with juice, has adjusted to the «climats». Not only to the glowing autumns which give rise to the northernmost great red wines in Europe, but also to specific biotopes which mean that the same variety of vine on the same soil will produce a different flavour from ten paces away. The vine's enemies, rain, frost and hail, do not strike in every part all at once and

▽ *The jewelcase: the vines of the Côte de Beaune.*

▷ *Mary and the
Wise Men:
tapestries of the life
of the Virgin
(Notre-Dame,
16th century).*

▷ *The porch of
Notre-Dame
presbytery.*

with the same consequences. In the olden days, they used to fire rockets to fend off disaster ; what a fireworks display rose up from the villages! Then they tried seeding clouds with an aeroplane. None of this proved conclusive. Beaune, like a good winegrower, lives with its nose to the wind, the master of its hard labour ; its Hôtel-Dieu is crowned with fifty gilt iron weathercocks.

The Gods

The Gods arrived at the dawn of history. Celtic horsemen with their long iron swords rose up from the East, five centuries before Christ. Very soon there was a crossing of tracks at the foot of the hillside, and priests around the sacred fount of Belena. It took its name from Belenos, the god of spring waters. The marketplace brought about by the pilgrimage became Beaune.

Then Caesar came along with the Roman pantheon. Belenos became Apollo, but was barely more latinized than his worshippers. Later, the soldiers of the VIIIth «Augusta» Legion nearly

imposed the bloodthirsty cult of Mithra, but the wild god of dark Egypt disappeared with the warring foreigners.

During the 4th century, Saint Martin himself preached another religion from the Orient, Christianity. With the support of the imperial power,

cast in ancient tradition - the bishop was at Autun, at the foot of Bibracte, whence the Eduen Druids had governed the Beaune region - bringing new hope, it rapidly spread. The ramparts of the castrum at Beaune were rebuilt «out of the rubble of the pagan temples». The first sanctuary rose up near the sacred spring.

During the 5th century, the Barbarians crossed the frozen Rhine. The Burgundians gave their name to the region, but abandoned their gods. One of their princesses, Clotilde, would marry Clovis. In the mid-8th century, the Arab incursion was no more than a razzia. Our Lady reigned over the town. The light of Christianity would illuminate the centuries.

Rediscovering the Old Gods

The Beaune site was inhabited even before history began. Down the ages civilizations came and went. You can relive this past at the Beaune Archéodrome on the Beaune-Merceuil rest area on the A6 motorway). Each year 200,000 visitors visit this the only facility of its kind in Europe. Constructed under the supervision of well-known scientists, this park uses all the resources of audiovisual technology and the charm of a Gallic farmhouse in this evocation of the past. The magic of the dark ages inhabits this place.

The Men

A cross-roads, passing place and market, Beaune received all kinds of contributions, from Roman and Syrian merchants, Greek and Parthian freemen, German and Dacian slaves. But the base stock was Celtic. It was a gradual melting pot of blood and souls. With the start of the second millennium, the many surnames Germanized during the reign

△ *Townsfolk in the 15th century: fresco at Notre-Dame.*

◁ *Two traditional trades on the marketplace today: left, the pork butcher; right, the gingerbread maker.*

of Queen Brunhild - Nibelung, Hildebrand, Gerfred, Amalsind etc. - gave way to new names. Through their history of the names of the people of Beaune, nominal tax censuses carried out by the Capetian dukes tell the story of the town itself and its seven faubourgs.

Neighbours' malice or naiveness often inspired nicknames - Jolyot, Traigneau, Mignotteau, Boitoux, Manquée, Sornois, Tranche-Coste, Gros Yeux or Bien-Garny. They bring back to life a whole population in all its poverty, truculence, its vices and dash. sickly Huguette, hungry Philippot, the Ramenant au Loup, Parisot the charmer, Jaquote la Trye, sworded Robin, kindhearted Symonot, Jehan of the vines and Jehan of the sky. Perhaps these young people whom the Duke's census takers named Pretty Jehan and the Charming Girl met each other ? Very soon, among the vigorous nicknames: Camus Musardet, Prince, Coillefrite, or the Gaul Henri Vincenot is said to have loved, tradenames dominate : Vigneron (Vinegrower), Tonnelier (Cooper), Charpentier (Carpenter), Lainier (Woolworker) etc. A people was born, a people of workers.

Some made a fine fortune, in cloth, wine or the legal profession. There would be - and still are - middle-class dynasties destined

to be aldermen and magistrates, the masters of the inner workings of the town. But little in the way of aristocracy nor the most brilliant either. The Gallo-Roman «clarissimae» whose luxurious domains carved up the Beaune region had other successors : the regular orders and the collegiate chapter. The Revolution and the Napoleonic Code distributed property. But in Beaune, even the wealthiest were not inclined to show off. To discover the miracle of luminous architecture and refined interiors, you need to go beyond the windowless walls and dark corridors.

Markets and Merchants

During the Middle Ages Beaune was a town of drapers. Long before wine, the textile industry made it rich. The now wooded hilltop was then wild moorland grazed by great flocks of sheep. Some of the wool was exported to Italy, the rest processed at Beaune. The quality of produce was stringently controlled. We know of one clever merchant who invented a «cloth stretcher» and whose yard of cloth measured on purchase promptly shrank once sold... The guilds came down firmly against fraud ; even the duchess, Margaret of Flanders, who would have liked to sell her Germolles wine using the Beaune label, failed to obtain permission to brand her oak casks with the coveted «B». This tradition of strictness still survives and you can in confidence seek out antique dealers and cake shops, pedlars' stalls and famous merchants.

▷▽ *A shop window in the Antique dealers' village.*

▽ *Another marriage of the traditions of Flanders and Burgundy: gingerbread made of wheat and honey, known as Duchess Margaret's «boichet», and «cassissines», pastries flavoured with the dark blackcurrants of the Hautes-Côtes de Beaune.*

Beaune of the Hours

The last Master of the Temple

When the «Iron King» Philip the Fair's executioners had broken in both mind and body the last surviving Master of the order of Christ's Poor Knights, who for two centuries, from their fortress-convent of Solomon's Temple, had supported the kingdom of Jerusalem, the old man spoke : «My oath was taken forty-two years ago in the Temple chapel at Beaune, by Brother Humbert de Paray in the presence of Brother Amaury de la Roche and several other knights. I promised faithfully to abide by the Order's statutes ; the cloak of Knight Templar was placed on my shoulders....» Thus it was that in 1265 Jacques de Molay accomplished the rites of his profession, and perhaps learned the Templars' deadly secret. That year for the first time, Beaune heard the joyful sound of the six bells of the church of Our Lady.

The pilgrims flocked towards the churches. As they went up the street leading to St Flocel's Chapel, they always found flowers at the door. From the 10th to the 13th century, the amazement remained the same : after a long, exhausting walk, the freshness of the flowers and, under the transverse rib arches of the pre-Romanesque vault, the underground church where burned sweet-smelling wax. This was what «Paradise» would be like at the end of the hard life of the poor. The cobbled street has kept the name.

Notre-Dame church dominates the town. The heart and pride of the old town, the «Distinguished Collegiate Church», lately raised to the rank of basilica, was constantly enlarged and embellished. Today, Romanesque and Gothic additions give it strength and elegance. A dazzling series of 15th century Flemish tapestries tell the story of Mary ; a thousand flowers illuminate the landscapes, with saints dressed in golden brocades, and shepherds kneeling in the midst of their white lambs lend an ear to the voices of smiling angels...

◁ *The majestic porch of the distinguished Collegiate Church of Notre-Dame.*

▽ *The familiar rustic porch of the faubourg church of St Nicholas.*

△ *A vine grower of the Beaune region: St Vernier (Musée du Vin).*

▷ *The 15th century belfry.*

The Keys of the Town

King John the Good, who became heir to the Duchy of Burgundy, entered Beaune on 20th January 1361. The mayor and aldermen went out to meet him on the Dijon road and led him in procession to Notre-Dame which had been strewn with fresh straw. The king went up to the choir, surrounded by the clergy in golden copes to echoes of joyful hymns. There the mayor said to him : «Swear that you will keep our constitution in all its truth, our town's privileges, our franchises and immunities ; and lastly, all our freedoms bestowed on us or recognized by the Dukes of Burgundy.» The King of France, with one hand on the Gospels, said in a loud voice : «I swear to spare your freedoms.»

After 1203, the «men of Beaune» were free. Duke Eudes III had made Beaune a free town. The town's seal, as broad as the dukes' great seal, represented in its field the picture of a girl with a long cloak over her shoulders, hel-

meted and sword in hand, standing amidst the ten «jurors». Behind the shelter of its ramparts and protected by its charter, the free town set about developing itself. Marauding lords, old Anglo-Navarrese troopers and brigands from the great companies were all repulsed. When the look-out in the clock-

tower of Notre-Dame called out, the urban militia ran to take up arms ; villages burned in the plain... Canons of Our Lady, imperious merchants, «coalitions» of clothiers and wine-growers were hauled back into common law. Court cases were long drawn-out affairs with the people of Beaune, who were dreadful pettifoggers. The king, the dukes and their officers had to use infinite diplomacy or face starting a revolt. Their soldiers were left to camp outside the city walls...

So, much was at stake in town government. It would take a Homer to recount the story of council elections in Beaune. It all ended with a fine ceremony at Notre-Dame in a town seemingly reconciled. But before that, what polemicking, what riots, what displays of naked force, what wild accusations! In 1452, Beaune even had two mayors, Pierre Clémence and Jean Grignard. Whilst the vote count was being contested, the one who thought he had won was regaling his supporters with bread and cherries.

> ### The Virgin with Grapes
>
> In classical times, Beaune marked its seal and coat of arms with the image of the Virgin Mother, placing in her hand a bunch of grapes amidst a fine motto : «Causa nostrae laetitiae... Cause of our joy». But during the century of sceptics the aldermen, fearing that ill-wishers might attribute the joy of the Beaunois rather to the grape than to Our Lady, changed the motto to «Urbis et orbis honos... honour of the city and the world...»

The Cortege of Princes

Beaune's renown was a major headache for the town council. Many famous visitors came and the authorities made feverish preparations for them. Questions of precedence made things a great deal more awkward. The rank of each during processions and services, the visible proof of their influence and power, was a matter of fierce dispute. On such solemn occasions, whilst the bells of all five parishes and monasteries rang out, the whole town took to the streets and one half of Beaune watched the other half respectfully escorting the day's guests.

In 1656, the young queen Christine of Sweden spent almost a week in Beaune. Claude Dulas, a painter of repute and master of the covered market, had set up great panels bearing the coat of arms of the Vasas at the doors of his mansion. The order of feasting was grand indeed, with pigeons, pike, partridge, ox tongues and game. Four low fellows carried the queen's chair. «The music in procession was very simple, but noisy ; it comprised first four drums, then three drums, then one drum, then yet another drum, with two drums in reinforcement from Nolay bringing up the rear...»

Two years later, young King Louis XIV and his mother were welcomed to the town. Anne of Austria came to

◁ *Virgin with Grapes (16th century).*

▽▷   *From these windows, the people of Beaune watched the «Mandrins» (ruffians) go by ... Place Carnot.*

▽   *The Marriage. Tapestries of the life of the Virgin (Notre-Dame, 16th century).*

thank the Carmelite monastery at Beaune for the intercession of the Venerable Margaret of the Holy Sacrament, to whose prayers the fortunate (and long awaited) birth of the Sun King was to be ascribed. But this humble message was somewhat lost on him, for the revocation of the Edict of Nantes had disastrous consequences in Beaune, and is traditionally held to have heralded the ruin of the ancient cloth industry.

The Beloved Brigand

The children of Beaune still sing Mandrin's song:

«There were twenty or thirty
of us brigands in a band...»

The legendary smuggler had barely more than that number of companions late in the morning of 16th December 1754, when they captured the town. The alderman on guard duty at the Madeleine gate had gone off drinking with his company... Louis Mandrin was a handsome man, in his prime, dressed in grey cloth with a plush red jacket, silk tie and hat embroidered with gold. As he robbed only the State, he was admired by the lower classes. He set himself up at the mayor's whilst he counted the 20,000 pound ransom to be taken from taxes on salt and tobacco. The financiers were later full of reproach towards the mayor ; had he not had six of his best bottles brought up from his cellar to drink with that brigand to while away the time until the money had been counted out! At around four o'clock, Mandrin wrote out a receipt for the bags of gold and silver, mustered his gang and rode off to La Roche-Pot. The town guards seized a straggler they found asleep down in a cellar...

When it was all over, the watch was called out. After midnight, a huge din of trumpets heralded the civil police of Fischer's light cavalry and Rodan's dragoons. These now needed lodging. As it turned out, they failed to capture the beloved brigand himself, for he had gone off to pillage Autun, where he entered under the pious cover of a cohort of seminarians he had captured on the way.

Flamboyant Beaune

The Town of a Dream

Beaune's finest hours, the flamboyant hours, so intense that they seem to encapsulate its entire history in less than a century, unquestionably came in the time of the dukes of Valois. Its journey however has shown that long before - and after - the 15th century, Beaune built, prayed and created. The town did not just appear from nowhere at the bidding of the great dukes of the West. Nor did it go back to nothing. And yet its greatness, unique among all these towns of works and days raised up by Europe, was born out of those luminous years when it started out as the town of a dream.

It was the autumn of the Middle Ages. The «great death», the plague from the Orient, had carried off one man in three. The English, the brigands and the wolves looked after the rest. The Duke of Burgundy, a child of sixteen, was dead. Would Beaune and the duchy rejoin a harassed France in the long nightmare of the Hundred Years War ? In this new age of a world painfully giving birth to its Renaissance, Burgundy was to follow a different path. In contact with the most fertile regions of Europe - Flanders, northern Italy, the world of the Rhine, the country between the River Saône and the Morvan - was to encounter its destiny. Beaune, the old judicial capital, would become the seat of the well-nigh sovereign parliament of the Valois dukes, of one of their chancelleries, and the most sumptuous of charitable institutions. For a century it would live through a great adventure.

◁ *Turret in the Notre-Dame quarter.*

Beaune was unwilling to see this dream disappear. Its duke was dead, betrayed and murdered. Louis XI's troops occupied the duchy. Dijon had submitted ; Beaune revolted ; in 1478, Philip of Chaumergy led an uprising of the town and recognized the authority of John IV of Châlon, Prince of Orange, «lieutenant of Madame the Duchess of Austria and Burgundy in the countries on this side» whose squadrons from the Franche-Comté held the Saône border. The King of France took revenge by dispossessing Beaune of its parliament, which was transferred to Dijon. Although its lucky rival gained great benefit from this, Beaune it was that stayed the witness of a great dream.

A History within History

The Hundred Years War, the Armagnacs and Burgundians, the burning at the stake of Joan of Arc, Louis XI's struggle with Charles the Bold - all this is the history of France. It is only partly that of the men and women who, from 1360 to 1482, between the Saône and the Zuydersee, the North Sea and the Rhine, lived under four implacable Grand Dukes : Philip the Rash, John the Fearless, Philip the Good and Charles of Burgundy. Beaune lived through this «history within history». Along with Bruges and Ghent it passed from the last of the jousts to the first caravel, from the black plague to the light of Van Eyck, from the massacres of feudal warfare to the dawn of the Renaissance.

In 1364, the king of France entrusted the duchy of Burgundy to his fourth son, Philip, whom the English called the

▷ *The Prodigal Son. Tapestry from Tournai (16th century). Hôtel-Dieu.*

Bold since he had fought as a child at Poitiers : «Father, take care to right and left...» His marriage to Margaret of Male, heiress of Flanders, Artois and Comté, enabled him to set up a new state of Burgundy-Flanders which his successors extended to the whole of the Netherlands. A flamboyant edifice thus emerged from a Europe on fire. The Burgundian standard - a red St Andrew's cross on a white background - was flown from the yard of warships. Sovereigns and princes became companions of the Duke in the Order of the Golden Fleece. The encounter between the cultures of north and south produced a number of master-pieces. Saints spoke with God and mystics invented free examination. Merchants created capitalist mechanisms and crafts-men printing techniques.

Mistakes, misfortunes, this inability of men to back ambitious enterprises beyond a certain stage, ruined the construction. But the momentum was not lost. The great heritage appeared to weigh heavily on the frail shoulders of Mary, a girl of twenty. She gave herself to the Emperor's son, the Habsburg Archduke Maximilian. Their grandson would be Charles the Fifth... For five centuries the State of the Dukes of Burgundy had not included the old dukedom ; its successors were far away to the North and East. The page had been turned. But Beaune had received its luminous imprint.

A Town within the Town

There were numerous witnesses of this great era in Beaune : the belfry, at the top of which Philip the Bold had had built that revolutionary instrument from Flanders, the clock, freeing lay society from the Church's Time, measured by the seasonal rhythm of the offices of canonical prayer ; near the collegiate church, the Dukes' mansion, where the sovereigns held their parliament and kept the wine from their vineyards ; houses lowly or luxurious with their turrets, their watch towers, their sculpted windows. But it was the Hôtel-Dieu, an almost unreal masterpiece, that embodied the flamboyance of Beaune.

It is a town within the town. Here the architecture offers the most subtle

▷ *Higher, lighter, richer than the palace of princes: the Hôtel-Dieu's «Grande Salle des Pôvres» (poor room).*

△ *Hôtel-Dieu. Door-knocker.*

◁ *Hôtel-Dieu. The courtyard.*

▷ *The large towns of Burgundy of the time were Lille, Gruges, Ghent, Brussels, The Hague, Dole, Dijon and Beaune. In about 1440 Rogier de la Pasture of Tournai, who worked in Flanders under the name Van der Weyden, created this masterpiece for Nicolas Rolin: the Last Judgement.*

contrasts. You enter through an unassuming doorway in the long bare facade of a huge ship covered with dark slates. The courtyard dazzles with the colour of the varnished tiles and the lofty skylights, gables and galleries. The heart of the Hôtel-Dieu is the great «Salle de Pôvres» (Hall of the Poor), with beds enabling the sick to follow the liturgy, draped on feast days with Flemish tapestries. The polypty-

▷▷ *The unmoved witness to the tragic, truculent and glorious hours of Beaune, the clock tower of Notre Dame watches over the town and vineyards.*

ch of the Last Judgement by Roger Van der Weyden above the altar was opened during Holy Hour. A Christ of pity gazed mournfully upon this vessel of suffering sailing onward to Paradise.

The Hôtel-Dieu design was based on a Flemish model and bears the mark of the wealthy Northern counties. But it is also Burgundian in its stone, its oak timbers and brilliant tiling. With its back to the ramparts, it is raised upon huge cellars, near tall storerooms - well anchored in the earth of Beaune, born out of the soil and its «climats», inseparable from Mother Earth. From a tall steeple, prayer rises up heavenwards, and lest God forget man, under the bell-ringer's fists, bells cheerfully peal out the old songs of hope and love.

Inside, very appropriate for the purpose, beauty abides in every little object – pewter jugs, the pharmacist's earthenware jars, the bed covers. Even the picture tiles on the floor are part of the work of art. In the large kitchen, the copperware shines and an automatic roaster seems to turn the spits. The emotion that overcomes the visitor doubtless comes from the enigma that this constant search for perfection represents for us in a place given over to serving the most sorely afflicted and poverty-stricken. We understand luxury in princely palaces and gold on altars, but where do we house our poor ? The Hôtel-Dieu at Beaune, this town within the town, is also a city from another age.

The Archangel's Judgement

In those days, men were neither ashamed of illness nor afraid of death ; they only feared for their souls. The soul of the wealthy having ever been in greater danger than others, charitable foundations were richly endowed. The chan-

The Sisters of Charity:
◁◁   *the kitchen,*

◁   *the spinning wheel,*

▽◁   *the linen store (far right, a novice).*

A community of nuns from Valenciennes was established in perpetuity in the service of the sick. Gentleness and humanity would govern the slightest detail of daily life. Each day white bread was distributed at the door of the Hôtel-Dieu. When at the supreme tribunal the Archangel calls Nicolas Rolin and his wife Guigone de Salins, the testimony that may tip the terrible scales will perhaps be that of an exhausted old woman - whose name will be known to the Archangel - submissively crossing the Passage from suffering to joy with her gazed fixed on the Prophets and the Chosen Ones of the great altarpiece.

The Future of the Past

This time of fear and challenge has long since passed. And yet the chancellor's foundation is still alive. The Hôtel-Dieu itself takes in old people, working hand in hand with a modern hospital and its specialist departments.

cellor of the Dukes of Burgundy, Nicolas Rolin, had accumulated great riches that made him hate men ; well could he fear divine Judgement. He decided to hand over some part to the poor, that is to God. The elder statesman, who had bartered many a betrayal and great act of repentance, knew he could bargain with princes but not with God. So when he chose Beaune in preference to Autun, his birthplace, to raise a hospital, he founded it with infinite respect for the poor, who can only receive as a necessity perfect beauty.

tic. They felt that a capital that had become a mere provincial town was bound to lose part of its soul. After rising up in the name of «Madame Marie», Beaune appeared to accept its fate. But one cannot break with a great past with impunity. The taste for feasts and processions is doubtless more than just a show ; this town where Nicolas wanted that «works of mercy and piety should be magnificently accomplished» in his Hôtel-Dieu has the tenacious will to be, rather than to last.

Nearly every year, it receives donations. Its highly profitable winegrowing domain finances building work and equipment. The «Sisters of Charity» are still there, having exchanged their mediaeval hennin for the nurse's veil. Their presence is like a sign of mercifulness.

Beaune is greatly attached to its Hôtel-Dieu. During the Revolution, as elsewhere marked by tremendous destruction, the clubs did not dare disfigure it. At the Chartreuse de Champmol monastery near Dijon, the duke's mausoleum was desecrated, the graves opened, the bones scattered. The paintings of the masters of Sienna and Flanders, the illuminated manuscripts, the crystal reliquaries were all auctioned off. Claus Sluter's great Calvary was overturned and the church taken to pieces. But at Beaune, the poorhouse was mostly left unharmed. Maybe after all, the real masters of the world are not those one might think...

What memory does Beaune keep of its flamboyant age ? The historians of the last century were not too optimis-

▷ *Hôtel-Dieu. Surgical instruments. 17th century.*

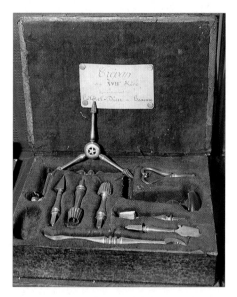

Wine as a Restorative

In 1727, Lordelot, the Hôtel-Dieu surgeon, received «each year half a hogshead of white wine to washe and mummyfie woundes». Apparently, if certain strange behaviour was anything to go on, he drank more of it than he used on the sick. Whereupon the authorities placed the fateful cask under the joint supervision of the apothecary, who was henceforth to take a personal part in preparing the lotions, and the nuns who were to hold it «under lock and key in a cupboard, along with the rest of the medicine».

The Count of Péluse

Beaune, in the days of Diderot's Encyclopaedia, had its scientists, its archaeologists, its geographers, many of whom owed their training to the Oratory Fathers.

Gaspard Monge was the son of a not very wealthy merchant from Beaune. When he was born in 1746, Louis XV was on the throne, and his armies were losing the Battle of Plaisance. The child did well during his years of study in his home town, and when he was sixteen, the Fathers offered him a post as physics teacher in one of their houses, along with the robe of their Order. But Monge, who had been spotted by an officer in the scientific arm of the Engineers for a plan of Beaune he had drawn, opted to teach mathematics and physics at the Royal School of Engineers at Mézières. There he wrote his Treatise on Descriptive Geometry. He was elected to the Science Academy sponsored by d'Alembert. On the eve of the Revolution, he was chairman of the examining board for naval cadets and hydraulics teacher at the School opened in Paris by Turgot.

All Monge was to retain from the storms of Revolution was the invasion of France. He accepted the Naval ministry after August 10th, then placed himself at the disposal of the Committee of Public Safety. Another officer with the Engineers, Lazare Carnot, born in Nolay a few leagues from Beaune, was in need of scientists to organize victory. Monge forged the artillery of the Republican armies. He spent his days in his factories and his nights writing treatises on casting cannon and technical manuals for steel workers.

As the foreign threat receded, Gaspard

◁ *Town hall: Abundance.*

▷ *Monumental staircase at the Oratorians college (17th century): another light on the paths to knowledge and freedom.*

▽ *Gaspard Monge by François Rude.*

Monge placed his genius in the service of the higher education which was to supply France with her scientific managers. As professor of descriptive geometry at the Ecole Normale, he organized studies at the new Ecole Polytechnique. This scientist was also a man of action ; when on a mission to Rome, he helped to found the Roman Republic upon the ruins of the Pontifical State ; Bonaparte took him to Egypt and made him President of the Cairo Institute.

Under the Empire, the poor Beaune merchant's son became senator for Liège and Senate President, Count of Péluse in Lower Egypt, President of the Institute and Grand Officer of the Legion of Honour. He devoted himself with great passion to the major work of his life, the Ecole Polytechnique. He would never forgive the Restoration, which hated the grandes écoles, for its temporary break-up.

Chronophotography

Étienne-Jules Marey began his studies at Monge College. His father, who dreamed of him becoming a physician at the Hôtel-Dieu, directed him to take up biology. He had an outstanding career as a physiologist. As «an engineer of life», he devoted his work to explaining organs and graphical representation of how they work. The imperfect techniques then available limited the application of his inventions. Nowadays with electronics, all their potential paths can be explored.

▽◁ *Étienne-Jules Marey (1830-1904).*

And yet, our admiration doubtless goes not to the President of the Academy of Science and Medicine and teacher at the Collège de France. Étienne-Jules Marey, who said of himself «I have only the memory of the eye», was first and foremost the man who changed our view of movement.

The Pompidou Centre in Paris devoted a fine exhibition to Marey's discoveries. Pontus Hulten showed how his work had dominated the century. Music, painting, sculpture, film-making all owed to him the final destruction of the plastic dimension of space handed straight down from the Renaissance and dominated by a world view based on the fixity of spatial relations.

The Beaune museum holds some precious collections, including collec-

ted works, descriptions of experiments and apparatus for analysing movement. Photographic documents produced solely for scientific purposes often attain the refined aesthetic quality of ideograms. Gaston Bachelard admired them for their poetry.

The White-faced Black Man

Xavier Forneret (1809-1884) was the most extravagant of French writers. He never left his home town of Beaune, where he lived in a ruined turret and slept in a coffin. The surrealists rediscovered his underrated work : plays, tales, novels and aphorisms. His books of poetry - *Untitled by a white-faced black man* ; *Vapours, neither verse nor prose* ; *A cretin and his lyre* etc. - are doubtless not worth that one remark which set André Breton dreaming : «One day I saw a letter box on a cemetery wall...»

---

*Chronophotography.
Marey Museum.*

Underground Beaune

The First Winegrower of the Dukedom

«I shall speak of the vine with the graveness that befits a Roman when dealing with the arts and sciences...» is how, in his solemn introduction to his Book XIII, Pliny proclaims that things to do with wine and the vine should be talked about seriously.

Beaune has a wine museum, the ancestor of every ecology museum in France, in the Dukes of Burgundy's residence, because that palace was also the house of the dukedom's first winegrower. As owners of the finest vintages in the cultivated land of Beaune, Pommard and Volnay, the dukes had the wines brought together by the tenant of their château. They made use of them with discerning taste. Convoys left regularly for their châteaux in the North. Flemish patricians, English wine merchants, bank agents from Bruges discovered their rich flavours, so different from

▷ *The Côte in autumn... Michel Tourlière. Tapestry. Musée du Vin.*

◁ *Hôtel des Ducs de Bourgogne. Now a Wine Museum.*

the sharp wines produced throughout most of Europe. The papal court in Avignon brought in supplies by «Saône boat». Petrarch accused the cardinals of committing the Pope to remain in Avignon for fear of being deprived of Beaune wine... In civilian struggles in France, in the councils' debates, «the Duke's wine» was a secret weapon in Burgundian intriguing. It brought prestige to the tables of princes. Philip the Good proclaimed himself «lord of the finest wines in Christendom».

Yet it was the first Valois who implemented the most coherent policy. He was

◁ A 13th century wine press. Musée du Vin collections.

a connoisseur. His wife, Margaret of Flanders, had set up a fine domain at Germolles and worked hard to promote it. Philip the Bold, taking great care to conceal his resolutions, sent for wine from Beaune when it was reported to him

▽ The «Mountain» and Côte de Beaune.

that the palace was out of all «but Germolles wine»... The Duke had his wine sold at the gate of the ducal mansion, visited his vineyards, oversaw his cellars. His practical experience inspired him to draw up a seminal document, the great Ordinance of 1396. In it we find a list, along with justification, of all the rules governing the quality of wine - respecting the calling of the soil types, selected vine stock, hard pruning, measured soil enrichment, grape-picking at precisely the ripe moment, careful wine-making, guaranteed vintage label. It is noteworthy that such strict principles

▷▽ *The wine harvest.*

are now upheld by a scrupulous and demanding profession.

The Wine Miracle

There is nothing quite so annoying as the recriminations that are made on occasion against the great wines, and to which the State can lend so obliging an ear. Their fame and the relative ease they procure for thousands of winegrowers is held to be due to some privileged situation. This lack of understanding dates back a long way : in 312, the rhetorician Eumenus wrote to the Emperor to defend his compatriots against the «pagus arebrignus» - from Beaune to Nuits Saint Georges - against envy and the tax authorities. The truth is more straightforward : hard work, technical ability and professional self-discipline make it possible to achieve high quality. It takes plenty of willpower to make good wine. To make poor wine, you can just let things slide...

All the wine professions have a share in its glory, winegrower, cooper, taster, salesman, cellarman and wine merchant alike. They are backed by a sizeable industry of winegrowing and winemaking equipment manufacturers, printers, packaging specialists and hauliers. Everyone in Beaune will talk to you about

wine, for it is the town's economic lifeline. Before being a celebration the fruit of the vine is the fruit of their labour.

In all the bookshops of Beaune, you will find the by now classic works by P. Poupon and P. Forgeot on the wines of Burgundy. Given their infinite diversity, such a guide is helpful. In Beaune itself, the winegrowing area covers nearly 500 hectares, divided into sixty «climats» or localities with evocative names that need interpreting. One Fifth Republic Prime Minister was astounded to be served «La Montée rouge 1968» (Red Rising) followed by «Grèves» (Strikes)! Names which actually evoke nothing worse than the Oxfordian marl on the surface along the edge of an ancient path and the dry, slightly sandy ground on the side of the Mont Battois. The rich presentation of collections of tools, costumes and wine-tasters at the museum in the Hôtel des Ducs will enlighten you on the «wine miracle», this gift from Beaune to the world.

◁ *Félix Ziem (1821-1911). Musée des Beaux-Arts.*

The Domain of the Hospices

The «Hospices de Beaune» in 1805 brought together the Hôtel-Dieu and the Charity hospice. Their traditional domain, increased through contemporary donations, is Burgundy's largest with 538 hectares of woodlands, 10 farms and 773 hectares of top vintage vineyards. Twenty-one «Hospices winegrowers» - an aristocracy - cultivate these noble vineyards. The year's wines are auctioned by inch of candle on the third Sunday of November. In 1995 Catherine Deneuve presided over «the world's biggest charity sale» : one 228 litre cask of Meursault on its own fetched 200,000 francs.

▽ *The cellars of Beaune: under their centuries-old vaults, the miracle of Burgundy wine is reinvented each year.*

Life Deep Down

Then you will meet it. You need to go underground. An underground Beaune with cellars as high as churches and with ridged vaults or humbler store-rooms, is like the counterpart of the visible town.

The Burgundian house always has a cellar for the wine to live and mature in. It must be neither dry nor damp, neither too high nor too low. Sometimes it has several floors in which the wines are gradually climatized at different temperatures. The cellars of Maizières Abbey near the belfry, those of the Chapter of Our Lady, those of the Cordeliers near the Hôtel-Dieu, are veritable monuments. Many are open to visitors. Beyond the iron gates and spiral staircases, under the vaults built into the rock, oak casks and tens of thousands of bottles are lined up.

But you will be in neither a tomb nor a warehouse ; here a living alchemy comes about. For in the spring, when the vines come into flower up there in the sunshine, deep down in the cellars, the wine vibrates and is moved : in Beaune they say «it remembers its mother»...

To Find out More

One of the four «Histories of Beaune» : the most charming, by Abbé Gandelot in 1772 ; the most erudite, by the archivist Rossignol in 1854 ; the rarest, by Joseph Delissey in 1941 ; the most accurate, alas unfinished, by Lucien Perriaux, an academic and mayor of Beaune, in 1974.

«The Chronicle of Works and Days in the Burgundo-Flemish State from Philip the Bold to Mary of Burgundy : when blazed the Golden Fleece» by Jean-Philippe Lecat, published by Fayard, 1982-1991 ; in Dutch : «De Bourgondische Uitdaging», Elsevier, 1985.

△ *The bastions have been turned into cellars: ten doors open onto the vineyards and the plain. But Beaune's most closely guarded secrets are safe within the precincts of the battlements.*

▷ *The cellars of the former Franciscan convent.*

Practical information

Key to Map
1) Tourist office rue de l'Hôtel-Dieu, Tel. 03.80 26 21 30; Minitel data terminal, 3614 BEAUNE. Guided tours all the year round.

Monuments Open toVisitors
2) Hôtel-Dieu (Hospices), rue de l'Hôtel-Dieu, Tel. 03.80 24 45 00, open all the year round from 9 to 11.30 a.m. and from 2 to 5.30 p.m. (in winter), from 9 a.m. to 6.30 p.m. (in summer). Unaccompanied or guided visit.
3) Burgundy wine museum, rue d'Enfer. Tel. 03.80 22 08 19, open daily, except December 25th and January 1st and on Tuesdays from December 1st to March 31st. Unaccompanied or guided visit from 9.30 a.m. to 5.30 p.m.

4) Fine Arts Museum (including works by Beaune artist Félix Ziem) and Marey museum, rue de l'Hôtel-de-Ville. Tel. 03.80 24 56 92, closed from November 2nd to March 31st ; otherwise open from 2 to 6 p.m. ; unaccompanied or guided visit on Thursdays at 3 p.m. by appointment.
5) Collegiate Church of Our Lady, open from 8.30 a.m. to 7 p.m.

Main Annual Events
Beaune International Baroque Music Festival : in July on Fridays, Saturdays, and Sundays in the Hospices court-yard or at the Collegiate Church of Our Lady. Auction of wines of the Hospices de Beaune : around the third Sunday in November, the «Three Glorious Days» of festivity, exhibitions, wine tastings and auctions.

Front cover:
The joy and passion of an architecture raised up at the cross-roads of civilizations: the Hôtel-Dieu (1443)

Inset:
Masterpiece of the soil and work of man: Burgundy wine.

Back cover:
Balance and invention of inner spaces : a courtyard in the Place de la Halle.

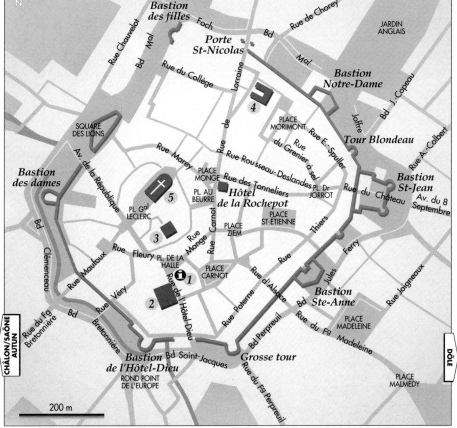

Cartography: AFDEC, Paris